Building Wealth

Proven Steps To Make The Most Money For Your Future

By Jacob William

Table of Contents

Introduction

In this book you are going to learn the steps it takes to build wealth to secure you and your family's future. Building wealth is something we all desire but so few people achieve. In fact, in America, it is said that only 1% of individuals make up 99% of the income. This may seem troubling to you and you may feel it is impossible to obtain such a goal. Although some of these individuals may have inherited their wealth, a good majority created their wealth from nothing.

You may not even desire to be in the 1%. Your goal may be able to create enough income so you can spend less time at work and more time with your loved ones. In this book you will learn what wealthy individuals do differently than everyone else. You'll learn what methods you can take to build your own wealth.

Remember wealth doesn't only have to be monetary. You will learn that contrary to popular belief, wealth means more than just how much money you have in your bank account. You will learn all the meanings of wealth and decide on which one correlates to you the most. Countless of people have used the steps in this book to build wealth for themselves and are now living the life of their choosing.

After reading this book, you will be able to jump right into action because you'll know exactly what steps to take to build wealth. You'll have a clear vision of what wealth means to you and what you will do to achieve your goals. You'll learn both traditional and nontraditional ways to reach the point in which you feel you are truly wealthy.

Is your goal to work less hours and spend more time with your family? Or to have enough money to travel around the world year round? Maybe you want to spend more time volunteering at your favorite animal shelter, or even spending most of your days on your favorite hobby. Whatever your goals are, just know it is possible for you or anyone else to achieve. You just have to have a clear vision of what it is that you want and this book will teach you step by step how to get there.

Stop waiting until New Years to make resolutions you never achieve. Start today and build the wealth you've always imagined because it is possible for anyone with a willingness to take action. Don't wait another day, or you'll be stuck living the same mundane life, doing work you can't stand. Continue reading Build Wealth: Proven Steps To Make The Most Money For Your Future, and watch how your life can change.

Chapter 1: Who Is Considered A Millionaire?

Contrary to popular belief, it's probably much easier to achieve millionaire status than you think. According to MarketWatch.com, by just saving $2,000 per year for seven years, a 15-year-old is capable of becoming a millionaire at age 65. A lot more surprising, that same teenager does not have to save another penny following the initial seven-year period, if the amount of money is invested properly. Amazing, isn't it?

Assuming you're over the age of 15, here's some more information which may be of interest for you. This is based on the assumption that you start wit $10,000 and increase by seven percent each year.

Age 25 = approximately $300 monthly until retirement
Age 35 = approximately $775 monthly until retirement
Age 45 = approximately $1,850 monthly until retirement
Age 55 = approximately $5,700 monthly until retirement

Taking a look at the big difference between each ten-year increment, you can see why you will need to start out saving for future years as soon as possible.

Read on to find out more of the best ways to get started on saving cash now. By the end of this book, you'll also learn several different tips to increase your income, in case you're considering storing even more. Let's begin.

Build a Budget

Creating (and sticking with) an acceptable budget is the main step to becoming financially secure. Yes, it's still possible to save lots of money without a budget. But, you'll find it is much better to save when you have at least a simple outline set up.

Track Your Spending Habits

Many people make the error of not tracking their income before they set up a budget. This makes the duty almost impossible to perform. You should know where your cash goes in order to get a grip on your present spending habits. Once you do this, it's easier to make a money management plan that you can live with.

It is important to remember that unless you track your spending, what you're going to be left with is a "wish list" of how you can spend your cash. Unfortunately, it will not take you long to determine that budgets don't work doing this and that even worse, you haven't accomplished anything.

Write it Down

Whether you decide to tackle your financial budget using a software or the old-fashioned way (with pen and paper), don't cut your expenses much that you take every bit of fun out of life. Be sure to put money aside for things such as entertainment and occasional splurges. Unless, you'll up throwing your finances out the window very quickly.

For instance, if you wish to eat out and do so often, don't completely cut it out from your life. Tell yourself you'll eat out once weekly instead. Alternatively, you can search the internet for copycat recipes of your chosen restaurant meals. You'd be presently surprised by just how many recipes can be found.

You may be wondering, what's the point? Well, when you make these dishes at home, you'll typically cut costs but almost 90% as opposed to going out. You can add this additional savings to your money box!

The simplest way to get started on tracking expenses is to create a list of categories you spend your money in each month:

- Rent/mortgage payments (homeowners insurance, misc. household upkeep)

- Health insurance

- Utilities (trash pick-up, water, cellphone, electricity)

- Car (gas, insurance, car finance)

- Food Shopping

- School (school lunches, tuition, sports)

- Entertainment

- Personal needs

- Credit cards/ other debt

This is by far a full list, everyone's budget is likely to be different. Take time to think about all of your necessary monthly expenses. Place each entry under the correct category. Next, work out how much you may spend on each category, within that same period. When you have any unusual expenses, simply put them under a miscellaneous category. You can always return later and make adjustments as needed.

Once you have completed that, it is time to work out how much money you pocket after taxes are paid. If you are having trouble each month affording to pay for everything you've listed, it is time to make changes in your life. If you are having trouble, changing things around to make it happen, you will need to cut some things from the budget. Other options include, getting a side job or coming up with new ways to supplement your income.

Financial experts advise that you save at least 10 % of your earnings each payment and placing it in secure places such as an IRA or 401(k) for long-term savings. If you like something more short-term, look at a money market funds or a six-month certificate of deposit.

No matter which option you choose, also make the effort to save some money with each payment. As the saying goes, if you don't see it, you won't miss it. Doesn't this make sense? With this method you are always sure to pay yourself first.

Financial experts also believe that 35 percent of your earnings should go towards housing expenses including rent or mortgage payments, utilities and more. Should your living situation allow you to allocate less then that, you're in an even better position. With this extra savings, be sure to sock it away into savings.

If available, an additional 10 % of your earnings can be placed away for a significant purchase like a new vehicle or your children's education. Based on what you plan on saving for, consider stashing it away in a college or university savings plan, such as a 529 plan or a higher interest-savings account.

If all things are aligned, you should be left with about 45 percent of your earnings, which could be considered discretionary income. It could go towards your other expenses or the best thing to do is to set it into an investment account. With an investment account you'll earn more passive income that will grow over time. This option is a better choice, rather than having it sit an a savings account with very little interest.

Chapter 2: Non- Traditional Ways to Save Even More Cash

In the previous chapter you learned what is actually meant when someone is considered a millionaire. Also just how simple it is to become a millionaire contrary to popular belief. It doesn't matter where you are in life at the moment. You too can become a millionaire.

One of the simpler ways is by saving your way to millions as discussed previously. With this method, it will take a longer period of time and discipline to reach the millionaire status. You will be required to set a budget and be frugal about spending.

In this chapter you will learn a few more techniques to help you build wealth in more non traditional ways.

Set Goals

Setting financial goals is one of the best things you can do in order to build wealth for the future. Many people aren't motivated to start putting money away, because they've never been taught how to proceed with it after they have it.

By the time they are of age or educated on the best course of action to take when it comes to saving money, they feel it is too late. It is never too late, the longer you wait, the longer it'll take you to build real wealth. Don't let time slip away, start taking action today.

Short-term goals can be easy to work through. Simply think about things that you want to have or spend money on, but are just out of reach financially. Once you have reached your goal, set your sights on the next thing.
While these goals can seem frivolous, the best short-term goals are the ones which helps further your career, in turn helping you increase your income. You can plan on saving for an online course, additional training, or even a certification which will help you excel in your career. With regards to long-term goals, consider what type of investments or purchases you would

make if you somehow won the lottery. Would you go out and buy the latest sports car or bring the business you've been dreaming of to life? If any of these ideas or other lofty goals sounds appealing to you, considering setting yourself up now financially for the future. Remember to keep the financial goals reasonable and steer clear of setting challenges yourself that you may well not have the ability to accomplish.

Together with your long-term goals set up, you could work out a financial plan that enables you to achieve these goals sooner rather than later, while still leaving you enough money to give attention to your more immediate wants and needs.

You'll know how much you should set aside every month and about how precisely long it will take to achieve your goal. With everyone having various situations, many people make an effort to set aside up to one-third of the income on a monthly basis. This can be difficult to do for some people, especially during hard times such as the holidays or if there is a financial crisis. However, saving if you're able to say one third or more of your income each month, you're going to be well on your way to building wealth quickly.

Take Every Job Seriously

It is important to take every job you have seriously, it doesn't matter how young or old you are. You never know what other opportunities may arise because of your job. Even if it is a job you aren't fond of or not your ideal dream job, never burn bridges. You never know what may come from it or who you may meet.

With each new position you take, you are learning new skills and gaining new experiences, even if it may not appear so. Typically one of two things may happen from these experiences. A few of the skills you learned may be new to you, no matter your level of education. Or, if the skills you learn aren't practical real life experiences, such as flipping burgers or faxing papers in a office. You may still benefits from these experiences by gaining references or even networking. Whatever the skills may be that you've gained while employed with your company, building the reputation as a hard worker and always willing to learn will take you far, at both your present job and future. On a brighter note, with all of that hard work and eagerness to learn, it might land you a bonus or raise amongst your co worker. This can then go directly to your savings, helping you build wealth.

Remember to always keep a good relationship with those around you. If your manager or supervisor likes your work ethics and you as a person, they may be able to help you get a higher paying job in the future. Remember, jobs always call your past employers as a reference. What they have been told about you can potentially have an impact on your future. Always work hard now and take your job seriously, to be sure their first impression about you is a great one.

Having a job that provides you contact with the general public also provides you an opportunity to create a network. For instance, a part-time job at a restaurant may lead to you acquiring buddies with business men who come in during their lunch time, who subsequently could put you into connection with people they know, if you are looking for a career change down the road.

Use Your Credit Wisely

Your credit history will follow you most of your life. It's vitally important to do whatever you can to safeguard it. Making proper use of your credit is among the smartest ways to make that happen. Unless you have good credit, you will be less likely to build real wealth in the foreseeable future.

If you are just getting started or a have a short credit history, you will need to develop credit. The only real way to tackle this hurdle is by using credit. You'll definitely have limited selections when it comes to getting approved for loans and credit cards. But, building your credit is a process that takes multiple steps.

Gas cards and big name retailers usually makes it fairly simple to acquire a new account. If you are in a credit union, a tiny personal bank loan might be also be a possibility.

You should try to only make a tiny purchase using one or two cards each month. Pay off your entire balance completely when it's due. This will help you build your credit and it also shows potential lenders your responsibility and that you are low risk.

During your lifetime, keeping a excellent credit score can save you thousands of dollars just in interest. Having good credit can also help factor in your buying decision when you are ready to purchase a house or in some cases even employment.

These are the top three mistakes to avoid in regards to your creditworthiness:

- Don't apply for too many accounts at once. This is a red flag to credit card companies that you are in desperate need for money and will take any card you can get.

- Don't max out your cards. A portion of your credit score is calculated by your credit balance. The lower the balance on your cards, the better to creditors.

- Don't close an account that you no longer use. This impacts the age of your credit. You want your report to show as long a history as possible.

Chapter 3: Diversify Where You Store Your Money

When it comes to building wealth, there are tons of different ways you can store your wealth. Some people only keep their money in a saving account and their jobs 401K. While these options are available, consider this, with a savings account you receive less than 1% interest each year. If you keep all your money in a savings account, you are actually losing money to inflation each year.

Your jobs 401K is a great starting point, but you can't withdraw money until a certain age or you will get a penalty. Again these are great starting points but there are other options to consider, in order to maximize the amount of wealth you build in the quickest amount of time.

Emergency Fund

Everyone should have an emergency fund with at least $1,000 tucked away. In the event that you feel as though this isn't possible currently because of your present income level, consider keeping at least $500 saved. Don't sneak and use this money for anything apart from an actual disaster. Taking money from this fund this cover an unnecessary expense or to cover one of your monthly expenses, will defeat the purpose of having an emergency fund.

U.S. Cost Savings Bonds

US Savings bonds no longer get as much publicity as prior times. This doesn't mean they're not a great option towards growing your savings account. US Savings bonds are considered a safer investment because they are covered by the government.

They are an excellent choice for any major purchases you may have in the future. With US bonds, you have agreed to put them in a safekeeping, for a certain amount of time and they typically offer more savings than a traditional savings account. Currently, the smallest amount you can purchase is only $25. Some people have been known to successfully use them as a supplement to their retirement income.

These bonds can also be used in combination towards funding your education. Keep in mind, a highly sought out degree can be instrumental for future financial security and wealth building. Having the right degree can help you land you your degree job which equates to more income.

Mutual Funds (Low-Fee)

Again, going back to the subject of long-term savings, it is time to discuss low-fee mutual fund. Low Fee Mutual funds , works great with insured deposits you might have accumulated. It is comprised of an assortment of stocks, bonds and extra non-deposit investments that are not covered by insurance by the FDIC.

The downside of low fee mutual funds is that in order to potentially have a higher rate of return, you must realize there is a risk of losing your funds if there were to be a financial crisis.

Health Savings Account

A health checking account or HSA is open to U.S taxpayers who are protected under a high-deductible health care plan. The amount of money added into this account is excluded from federal income tax. If the funds aren't used within a calendar year, they roll to the following indefinitely.

Increasingly more businesses are doing their part by adding to these employee health savings accounts. There is a limit to the amount that can contribute for both singles and families. This limit typically raises a bit each year.

During this time of writing, you can use these funds to pay for qualified medical expenses. You won't have to worry about a federal tax charges if you do so. It ought to be known, that medication can't be paid with this money unless there is a prescription from your physician.

If you look at this account, it may appear that it has nothing to do with saving for your future and building wealth. Look at it this way, over time if you use this account very little or even at all, all of these savings will eventually add up.

529 Plan

A 529 plan is a financial plan that gives tax advantages and other bonuses to individuals who are putting a kid or grandchild through university. The earnings of the 529 plan aren't subject to federal or state tax when used for tuition, fees, etc. for the beneficiary. You are able to name anyone as the beneficiary of your 529 plan, including yourself.

Benefit From Online Tools

Today, with so many online tools being offered (some even free of charge) by programmers, getting assistance with your personal savings or personal budget is really as easy as downloading an app on your phone. But, with so many choices available, it's likely you may find it difficult on deciding which app is best. Don't stress, though - here are two popular options available.

Mint.com

Mint.com is a free of charge website which uses software to help keep track of your transactions and presents you an outline of your finances. Mint links all of your personal finance information to keep track of the usage of your income. It can remind you to pay bills, advises financial accounts with better interest rates, and even lets you know your credit history.

Buxfer.com

Like Mint, Buxfer is a personal funding software designed for free to the general public. If you have the basic version, it is offered to you at no cost. More advanced features are offered to you but at a monthly cost. Buxfer offers more operation than Mint; however, it is no longer being backed by its programming team and probably will no longer have improvements during future updates.

Chapter 4: Pay Off Student Loans and Boost Your Income

Congratulations on obtaining your degree! It's never too soon to start thinking about paying back your student loans, or could it be? You may be surprised to discover that there are both benefits and drawbacks to paying back your student loans early. Ultimately it is up to you to decide whether this is the right move.

One of the best things about paying off your student loans early is you no longer have to take a portion of your money out to give to creditors. You can now put this money towards building wealth and you can begin to focus on new ways to boost your income.

You'll learn the pros and cons of paying off your student loans early and who is this best for. You'll also discover new ways to create more income for yourself.

The Pros

Repaying your loans early may seem to be rather costly as you begin paying it back. But it saves you more money over time. Paying the minimum amount every month, the interest builds up over time, which increases what it costs you to repay the debt. Alternatively, if you were to repay your loan completely off today, you avoid adding anything extra to the monthly bill.

In the event that you continue to make loan payments, you're trimming into your money flow. Although your monthly premiums are manageable, eradicating them leaves you with an increase of money to work with throughout the month.

Paying your loans off early, also decreases your debt-to-income proportion, or the quantity of your income you utilize to eliminate credit debt. That is helpful when you obtain a loan or home loan in the foreseeable future, as lenders take your debt-to-income proportion under consideration before they make a decision if you are approved.

If you cannot pay off all your student loan simultaneously, you might still want to consider attempting to pay it back quicker. Adding even a tiny total each payment can shave calendar months from your loan term, which causes you to pay less in interest.

This won't save any money initially. Actually, paying more every month will have an even bigger effect on your cash flow. But, after the loan is paid entirely, your finances will go back to normal.

The Cons

If you're also focusing on paying down other credit debt, such as bank cards or another loan, paying down an educational loan in full may not be your best idea. With regards to eliminating debt, focus on the lending options with the highest interest rate. The bigger a loan's interest, the more costly it'll be over a period.

Paying down any bank card before you handle the education loan also has a larger positive effect on your credit history. That's because education loan debt is an installment debt, this means it is made up of fixed repayments that should be paid during a set time frame.

Personal credit card debt, on the other hands, is a revolving debt. Which means that your debt changes from month to month as you buy things with (or repayments toward) your credit card. Revolving debts lingering on your credit file will decrease your score much more than installment personal debt will, particularly if you make all your installment payments on time.

Education loan interest, unlike the kind you pay to other lenders is tax deductible. Paying your student loan balances off completely could cause you to lose out on tax deductions. However, there's a limit to how a lot of this interest can be deducted, so execute a little research to see if this taxes break will be worth considering.

Completely paying your education loan off also isn't a good idea if doing this means spending everything in your savings or emergency fund. Whilst getting those debts paid can save you money in the long run, it's still important to have an emergency fund set aside in case of an emergency. It's far better to spend a little bit extra later than once you build your emergency account than to have no money at all when you truly need it.

Tips for Paying Down Your Education Loans

Add Payments. Reserve money halfway through the month that can go toward paying down your loan. While these payments do not need to be as large as a typical monthly payment, make an effort to pay as much as possible to see your loan payments be reduced quicker.

Write Out a Plan. Get out a calculator and workout how much you pay each month and exactly how soon the debt will be repaid. Should your finances changes (for better or even worse), you might consider re-working your plan. If this situation arises, understand you still want to come up with a way to pay as much money as you can be towards settling your balances. Writing out a plan also allows you to set up financial goals and stick to them.

Seek Other Ways to Make More Money. Be it money from a birthday, vacation or lottery, ensure you pay a little bit of your loan off each and every time you have the opportunity.

Setup a University Account. Have money automatically added to your account, it causes you to stick to the plan you decided on. Make sure with the new account, you will use these funds towards paying down your debt.

Look For a Part-Time Job. This may not bring in a ton of income but this will help dramatically in adding towards paying down your debt and building your resume to gain work experience. Depending on your major, some careers over programs to help pay off your loans when you work with them for an agreed upon amount of time. Make sure this is work you actually enjoy doing, or you will be miserable. This may lead to you quitting the job and not having your loans paid off.

Stay Focused. It could be very hard to stay disciplined as it pertains to your spending habits, especially while you're in school. Avoid the traps such as spending money on going out, buying clothes and other unnecessary expenses.

Maintain Low Expenses. Only spend money on items you need. Try and find a way to reduce the cost of these items. Such as your cellphone bill, groceries, household expenses and other necessities. The more ways you can find to cut back on these expenses, the more money you can put towards paying off your debt.

Stay Healthy. The less trips you have to take to see a doctor, overall you'll have less to pay towards co-pays, travelling and prescription costs. By keeping healthy, you can cut costs that can go towards your personal savings or paying down your debt. Here's some advice on how you can stay as healthy as possible.

Maintain a Healthy Diet Plan. The foods you eat have a huge impact on your overall health. To keep your system in good shape, it is important that you take in a balanced, nutrient-rich diet. Adding vegetables & fruits to any meals is a superb way to add plenty of nutrients. Dark, leafy greens is a great addition to any meal and are excellent for energy boost and overall health.

Be sure you include include healthy protein in your meals. Whether you choose to get your proteins from an animal or non-animal source, it is important that you take in the necessary recommended amount each day. Most people need 40-60 grams of proteins every day which can be easily obtained if you focus on a whole foods diet.

Your body requires water for maintenance of your entire body function. Make an effort to drink at least eight glasses of water each day and much more if it's a hot day or if you've planned very vigorous activities.

Get In Good Exercise. 30 minutes each day of weight training or cardio exercise will help keep you fit, strong and healthy. Try exercising and stretching early in the morning when you wake up to start your day off on the right foot. Over time as you become better at it, you'll start working out for longer than 30 minutes.

Physical exercise will leave your system feeling rejuvenated and packed with energy, even if it can first appear strenuous. Not only will exercising save money by keeping you away from the doctor's office, you might discover a fun, healthy hobby that can save you money on movie seat tickets or other entertainment costs.

Don't Neglect Sleeping. Based on the U.S. Centers for Disease Control and Reduction, thirty percent of American men and women aren't getting enough sleep. Typically, men and women need seven to eight hours of sleep every night, though a majority get less than six.

Ensure that you are getting enough sleep every night and that you have a regular sleep schedule. Sticking with a continuous sleeping schedule helps make certain you get restful sleep every night and that you are feeling refreshed and energized the next day.

Income-Boosting Tips

There are so many ways to make more money especially in today's day and age. With the creation of the internet you can make extra income from home or if technology isn't your thing you can always pick up a second job. Below are a few ways you can do to boost your income.

Rent Out An Area or Storage. While sharing liveable space might not exactly be an attractive option for everybody, you have the option to rent out your spare room. With sites such as airbnb, it has never been easier to make extra money without any extra labor.

Sell Unused/Unwanted Items. Not only is this a great way to make extra income, this is also a great way to clear up clutter in your home. With sites such as eBay you can easily post things online and sell them in a matter of minutes. For some, they've been able to make a full time living from selling items in their home and from stores.

Take on More Hours at Work. If you aren't interested in making money elsewhere and your job offers overtime, work those extra hours to make extra income.

Say Yes to Moonlighting. Obtaining a second (or third) job is a fantastic way to save lots of money for future years. Based on the Bureau of Labor Information, over 50% of individuals take on at least one extra job each year.

Consider Freelancing. If you have a skill you can offer your service to online, consider freelancing. The amount of freelance work is growing each year and has been said that ⅔ of workers will be freelancers over the next 10 years. Some in demand skills are coding, web design, freelance writing, bookkeeping, and so much more. Whatever you specialize in there is a job for it. If you don't have any particular skills, now is a great time to learn one to bring in extra income.

Start a Small Business. Do you have spare time and a passion for something you've always wanted to start a business in? Now is the best time to start one. There is nothing stopping you from turning that love into a way to make more income or one day even replace your day job.

52-Week Personal savings Challenge

The 52-Week personal savings challenge is typically brought up at the end of each year. Many people see this as a great New Years resolution to start saving more money. However, you can get started on this challenge any week of the year and end up with the same results, a supplementary $1,378 in your pocket

The first week you commit to save $1. The next week $2, the 3rd week $3 and so fourth. Continue doing this for 52 weeks, closing with a $52 deposit which you will end up with $1,378.

If you have extra cash, you can get a bit creative with this challenge. You can double your deposit. Week 1 start with $2, week 2 add $4, Week 3 add $6 and so fourth. Challenge your loved ones or relatives to this challenge to get everyone on board with saving more.

Write out your progress to keep track of the progress you've made. It has been say when you write out and see things, it is more of a motivating factor.

Save All your Change

It might seem silly to be told that saving all your pocket change can actually assist in securing a brighter financial future. But, if you constantly say your coins, you will see how much it adds up in the end. This doesn't apply to you if you usually pay with a card. However, if you purchase a lot of things with cash, this approach is something you should really take into account.

As clique as this may sound, you won't to go out and buy a piggy bank. Be sure and buy the ones that are hard to open, that way you won't be sneaking into the jar for those quarters.

Chapter 5: What Is Wealth?

Whenever you hear the word wealth, what is the first thought that comes to mind? Someone who owns a yacht, name brand clothing, a house by the beach? To numerous individuals the world wealth implies having lots of money and the possibilities in life being endless. Contrary to popular belief, if we actually delved deeper into the word, we would see that wealth is much deeper than materialism.

If we look at Merriam- Webster dictionary, the definition of wealth reads, "abundance of valuable material possessions or resources" A portion of this definitions alludes to monetary abundance, however the other half appeals to resources. From this definition alone, wealth not only means you are cash rich but you are rich in resources which doesn't necessarily mean monetary or physical possessions.

If we know wealth is more than monetary, why do some people think his or her possessions make them wealthy? This implication depends on the individual. You know that wealth is more than monetary having wealth includes, great health, new and exciting life experiences, healthy relationships, lasting memories and so much more.

Wealth is all about perspectives. What you may consider desirable may differ from the next individual but that doesn't mean what you want isn't consider wealth or vice versa. Happiness comes from within and whatever you desire in life you can achieve.

Some examples of what wealth can mean to you is, finding your soulmate, raising a large family, going to your favorite vacation spot every year or pampering yourself at the spa every month. Think about everything you desire and write it out on a piece of paper so you can see it everyday. Read this list every morning when you wake up and right before going to sleep. This is how you can create abundance in your life.

Anything you desire is possible, ANYTHING! Think deeper than money and material possessions. Think of the lifestyle you want to live, the people you want to be surrounded by, the impact you want to have. This is when you you'll truly become wealthy.

Always Have A Long-Term Perspective

When you near the end of your life, imagine everything that you will be thinking. In your deathbed, will you wish you had more designer clothing or a more expensive car? Or will you wish you spent more time with your children, loving your partner , spending more time outside and less time stressed at work?

Whatever will come to mind then, is what you should spend the most amount of time pursuing now. Don't be distracted on your phone while your loved ones are speaking to you, really take in what they are saying. The words they speak will mean more than what ever distarcion you are paying attention to on your phone. Take in the views while you're on vacation, don't always run to social media. Live in the present and don't get so caught up on past decisions and what things that hasn't even happened yet in the future. If you hate the situation you're in, you can always change it, you aren't a tree.

Of course it's okay to spend time on social media and plan for the future , but don't let these things consume your entire existence and distract you from your goals.

Pass This Perspective Along to the Next Generation

Whether you have one child, some children, or you hold some form of influence over those in the next generation, you can teach them these values on wealth building and abundance. There is always a need for positive role models in our children's lives that will teach them how to lead the way.

Remember wealth means more than having a bunch of zeros in your bank account. You want to let your children know this so they don't spend their adolescents chasing money for material goods, but are instead pursuing something of value. It's easy for the next generation to get distracted and attached to the wrong ideas especially with how technically inclined they are and how consumed they are with social media. Having this talk with them is just as important a conversation as any other you would normally have.

Remember kids model what they see and what you do means more than what you say. Spend more time living the life you want for yourself and less time slaving away at a job just for a paycheck. Volunteer for causes you believe in. Really spend time with your family, friends and ones you care for. Truly live in the moment and spend time putting your energy into the people surrounding you rather than things.

Be sure to make time for your favorite hobbies, invite others along to make it more interactive experience. You would be surprised at how much of an impact you have on others simply by offering your time and conversation. As you take more time to do the things you enjoy, spend more time with the ones you love and overall make the best effort to live in the now, people will take note and see the wealth within you.

Remember wealth is bigger than yourself and you must take the time to lead by example for the next generation.

Identifying What Truly Is Important

As you figure out what you consider wealth in your life, you can start by distinguishing your needs and choosing what is vital to you. To do this, take a seat when you have the chance to unwind and focus regarding the current matter.

Start by considering, and afterward record which things throughout your life you completely couldn't live without. Consider the things you have that you are appreciative of. Ponder on the things you don't yet have that you really wish to sometime in the not so distant future. Create a list of the things that put a smile on your face, and lights up your life.

Those that keep coming to your mind and things that continue striking a chord are those that will be on your list of what you consider to be true wealth. There aren't any rules to the way toward deciding true wealth, and your list may cause different emotions, feelings, and experiences.

When you realize what is essential to you, you can choose how you will benefit as much as possible from this list. Realizing what is important to you does nothing for you unless you follow up on it. Create a plan of action
to reach those goals and start taking those steps.

Stop delaying the process. Although wealth is more than just money, sometimes cash can help encourages us to achieve our actual non-monetary objectives. In the event that you require cash to achieve your objectives, you need to start saving. Make an arrangement to set a specific sum aside, and reward yourself when you achieve little objectives. This will enable you to get to the place you wish to be.

Chapter 6: Appreciate What You Have

Wealth is everything in life that you cannot live without. It really is those ideas near and dear to your heart and soul that provide you inspiration, determination,drive and desire to live life well.

Even though we aren't focusing on materials things, however, we can still get swept up in attempting to acquire increasingly more of something. Whether our top priority is family time or making memories, resist the enticement to simply want to rack up your experiences. This defeats the reason as much as concentrating on becoming economically well off.

The best way to combat this trend towards selfishness is by appreciating what you have. Whenever you make a spot of simply having a feeling of appreciation for all you have, you will see that all you acquire in the future looks even sweeter.

One severely forgotten source of prosperity is the prosperity of meaningful human relationships. Money cannot buy the sort of good, solid connections that add value in your daily life. Arrange your priorities on people and do what you can to foster these sort of relationships.

Having good, sturdy and sound friendships with others enriches your wellbeing, and can truly add years on your life. With the support of a good group of folks who is there for you through heavy times and thin, become familiar with about all the concealed intricacies that life provides. This is the sort of enriching situation that people should view as true riches.

It is important to always appreciate what you have in life. You can always have it worst. Below are a few ways to appreciate what you have.

Have a Gratitude Journal

There are various ways someone can appreciate what they have got. A thing that many therapists recommend is keeping a gratitude journal. Once you take into account the good stuff in your daily life, write it in your journal.

Keep the journal and pen convenient to enable you to write down thoughts as they come to your brain during the day. Keep a particular section on your smartphone to jot it down as it involves you each day, and then transfer it by the end of every day. The act of copying it in a handwritten journal is important because you will notice your list grow in a single place, which is therapeutic to employ a journal rather than keeping everything on your pc or smartphone.

Another smart way to understand what you have is by beginning and ending on a daily basis with thoughts of gratitude. Print some of your selected quotes concerning gratitude and post them beside your bed as a reminder.

As you may wake and commence every day, and before you drift off at night, utilize this as a chance to meditate on all the beautiful blessings in your daily life. Take into account the many things you need to be grateful for, and let yourself awaken and drift off to these thoughts. That is a terrific way to set your brain in to the mode of gratefulness, also to focus your ideas on the sort of wealth that is actually important.

Write Thank You Notes

Another strategy to help you appreciate what you have is to create notes of thankfulness often. Set an objective, such as you will card weekly, and hold yourself to ultimately do this. Every one of us have more and more people inside our lives that deserve our thanks, and sending them an email has gone out of the normal and can brighten their day.

A lot of people are so encouraged by way of a handwritten note of thanks that they keep these notes permanent rather than let them go. Maybe your aunt invited you to a great barbecue, or a pal was extremely generous in times of great need. Maybe you remember a school teacher from way back when who made a deep effect on your daily life. Whatever the reason why, discover a way to let these folks understand how much it means to you.

To make your thank you notes even more unforgettable, add a photography of you enjoying the fruits of the person's sacrifice. It'll be sure to place a smile on their face and can cause them to become be kind and generous towards others as well.

Share with Others

Another smart way to figure out how to appreciate what you have is to provide to others. Whenever we live our lives taking rather than giving, it is similar to a bowl that has water constantly running in it rather than out. It is going to have to overflow onto others. Let this overflow be the right path of passing it along to another individual, who'll hopefully pass it along over and over.

Even though you aren't materially wealthy and cannot give a sizable sum of money financially yet, you can give from what you have. You may treat your sister with an ice cream cone if you are at the retail center, or possibly you can transfer your old guitar to a, talented child who's understanding how to play it.

Giving with this type of generous heart will usually get back to you somehow, in an optimistic way. Let yourself live a life of abundance. Giving is one of the better ways to get this to a reality.

Appreciate the Tiny Things in Life

Noticing the tiny things is an instant way to rack up your appreciation for the life span you live and the wealth within it. Don't just await the feelings of appreciation to come when you acquire that big object, relationship, or experience. Allow tiny things and occasions you face everyday to have provoke feelings of happiness.

The sensation of your son or daughter's soft hand holding yours as you walk outside, just how fresh corn on the cob bursts in the mouth area as your teeth sinks into it, and the smell of your essential oils through your diffuser each morning are things that you will be thankful for. It generally does not have to be something bigger than life to understand it thoroughly.

Chapter 7: Does Money Buy Happiness, and Just How Much Is Enough?

Does money buy happiness? Well, it depends. If you're unhappy, no sum of money will help you. However, money can solve certain issues that can cause stress and suck the joy out you.

In the quest for our dreams and our need to exist to the fullest, we occasionally get swept up in the corporate jungle of maintaining everybody else financially. Just stop it. Constantly Spending money on friends and family is never going to enable you to get long-lasting joy or peace in virtually any sense of the term. True feelings of joy and gratefulness are brought by knowing what you have and being thankful.

The purpose of making money shouldn't be only to gain more of it, but instead to have the ability to generate a cushion all around us which allows us never have to worry about day-to-day issues. Whenever we find ourselves with a good amount of financial wealth, additionally it is our responsibility to spread it around. Contribute to friends and family in need, or a charity of your decision, it creates no difference who you share with. The main point is only to give when you have, to whatever brings us a feeling of great joy.

Understand that you will realize you reach monetary success when the money you've acquired, causes you more trouble than the joy it brings you. When you have problems with your investments, or you start attracting individuals in your life only because of your money, you might have reached a tipping point. If you ever reach this point in your life, it's time to switch your mentality and focusing on contributing to causes you care about.

Get to the point in your life where you are holding employment doing work you like and providing for your own as well as your family. Draw the line when you are feeling overworked and no longer in a position to enjoy what you have. Say no to additional income when it's going to hinder your loved ones life or essential personal time.

A portion of maintaining balance in life is due to addressing the issues we can deal with, and choosing never to let other things steal our joy. If the key problems in your daily life are caused by something you can transform, you should change it.

For instance, if you've gained weight and can't enjoy playing sports because you're on your computer all day at work, try to make changes that may help you live a more active rather than sedentary lifestyle. Create a workout regimine you enjoy, and make small changes in your diet. This sort of problem is well within your control and you certainly ought to do what you can to bring more joy into your daily life.

If you had a personal injury that triggers severe pain which causes you to sit out for your favorite sports, then do what you can to heal the injury, but recognize that the results may be somewhat out of your control. Give yourself time to heal and reflect but don't consistently beat yourself up.

During this time of healing you can focus on other areas of your life you may have disconnected from. This might involve reconnecting with your faith, or reconnecting with old friends. Choose habits that will donate to your mental well-being, such as daily meditation and regular time for relaxation.

If you feel there are things you can improve on in your daily life, then decide on what it is and make plans to tackle these changes. You don't have to overwhelm yourself, simply use your list as helpful information whereby you can implement one change weekly or in whatever time frame fits you best.

For instance, if you live a busy life and constantly feel overwhelmed with stress more often than not, think of the changes you can create in your daily life that could make a positive impact on your wellbeing. A few changes you can consider are, creating a normal bedtime plus a night time routine, reducing your time allocated to social media, building the body and mind by participating in a relaxing exercise such as yoga, and making time for friends at least one time per week.

When you yourself have been blessed with plenty in virtually any area, discover a way to give back again to others also to pay things forward. "Paying it forward" is the act of giving to someone from what you have been given. You can certainly do this through random acts of kindness, which is actually doing something nice for a stranger rather than expecting anything in exchange. Whether you have a surplus of money, time, or resources, make it a habit to lift others up who lack for some reason.

When you have been blessed with health, make use of it to help those who find themselves sick. When you have money, contribute to those who find themselves in need. When you have more time, offer to help a pal who has a great deal to do rather than plenty of time to take action. Giving can be financial, but it can even be hanging out volunteering, making things for others with your personal talent, or baking meals for a fresh mom or children where someone is ill.

Wealth is popular by many, but all too often we seek the incorrect things. So that they can become wealthy, a lot of people look for the profit that can make them feel accomplished in life, when they must be looking inward instead. In a society where most are lacking in what matters, make it your goal to build up the sort of wealth that will in actuality enrich your daily life, and the life span of these around you.

Pursue Your Passions First

Money shouldn't be your first priority. Having some financial wealth to fall back on can make life easier sometimes, to be certain. But putting it as your first focus will disappoint. Forget about making the most money and opt to pursue your passions first, then true wealth should come to you.

Think first about the person who chooses a job predicated on the salary offered to them. He gets his education, finds employment and commences to work. He doesn't love what he does but it earns him ample money so he keeps at it. He spends his entire week getting excited about the weekend as his soul is slowly sucked out of him.

He can't wait to finish work every day and then for the weekend, and he dreams non-stop of retirement. His health declines from the strain of working full-time at employment he despises. Whether or not he makes enough money to live a life very comfortably, the amount of money won't bring him wealth or true happiness.

Now think about the person who chooses to pursue training and employment in a job that he really wants even if the pay isn't that great. This man will love his education as he's studying what he feels interested in. He'll then find employment in the field where he can spend some time doing what he feels compelled to do. Although the job may have its challenges and downsides, he'll have the ability to stay with it because it is exactly what he loves.

This man will have a larger tendency to physical and mental health, and he'll have the motivation to remain strong when he's feeling weak. Pursuing your passions is usually a good choice, even if you aren't making all of the money in the world.

Things That Kill Our Appreciation For Non-Material Wealth

There are a few toxic thoughts and activities that can make it impossible to attain non-material wealth, or at least can make it challenging. Avoid these by any means, because they are things that will distance yourself from true happiness in the long run.

Although almost all of these has plagued most of us at one time or another, the secret is to distance away from them and not to entertain them when they come around.

Materialism

One of the biggest offenders in this category is materialism, since it has a means of constantly pulling you back again to what's bringing you profit but slowly chipping away at your happiness. It's the voice within you that lets you know that you should stay later at the job even though you aren't being fairly compensated just so you can buy that outfit. Sometimes this voice will even encourage you to get an unnecessary second job in order to buy those material goods.

There's always a balance in life, which is sometimes why it's the most challenging. You of course do need to work your hardest and do your very best, it could be difficult to justify taking things easier. But getting off-balance and working too heavily is merely as detrimental as no longer working by any means. Work hard, then put as much of yourself into your time and effort resting.

Bitterness

Bitterness is another example of a appreciation killer. If you're not grateful for the money you have the people in your life and the and activities you can partake in, it'll lead to envy of what others around you seem to be to have the ability to gain so easily. Jealousy will blind someone to the blessings that you do have.

The best way to overcome this is to produce a conscious effort to be grateful and thankful for what you have. Find different ways to include gratitude into your daily life. You may want to invest into a gratitude journal and spend daily time reflecting on the events that unfolded that made you feel safe and happy. You could even have another person make a list of all the qualities they love about you. The more you show gratitude, the greater it will seem to be that positive situations are attracted to you, subsequently providing you even more to feel thankful for. It really is a win-win situation.

Apathy

Just one more attitude that is quite capable at squashing the opportunity at true wealth is apathy. This is actually the silent killer. Apathy will cause you to care very little which will deter you from growing. It'll make you feel like you are unable to change lives anyhow, why even try? It'll pick away at you until you are feeling completely useless rather than willing to go even a step of progress. Make sure to weed this out before it eats away at your dreams and infringes on your own future.

Chapter 8: The Road to Pursuing Inner Peace

Inner peace is vital in discovering your own version of wealth. It really is in itself a kind of wealth. When you yourself have peace, you'll be able to navigate life's toughest circumstances without feeling uncontrollable. Even though times are tough, you will feel as if it is possible to make it through.

To find this type of peace, turn to your faith as well as your relationships. Faith is important as it'll help you when even your friends and relations have failed you, which can be a common occurrence. Look for the deeper meaning of life.

Consider who you truly are inside and find out your greatest qualities. These qualities contain the key to your daily life calling. When you yourself have found the reason that you exist for, it'll be much easier to remember your grounding when you are feeling as if you have lost the right path. Inner peace is actually one of life's greatest resources of pure wealth. When you yourself have found it, snatch it rather than letting it go.

Finding True Wealth

When you yourself have started on the journey to locating true wealth, you will see changes which may have to be produced. Don't rush them, because these necessary changes will continue to work their own way into existence.

Life offers ample opportunities to grow and change. If you don't learn your lesson the first time, you can be certain that you'll have to learn the same lesson over and over until you have decided to make the necessary changes to move forward in life.

Understand that this same phenomenon is happening to everyone. Don't delay, although you may fear the amount of change that will occur in your life. If you no longer want to go through the sae hardship over and over again, choose to learn and grow. Otherwise, you risk becoming trapped the same spinning wheel that will never end.

Wealth is one of the highly most misunderstood words throughout time. Wealth has often been used to symbolize status, glory and popularity. True wealth, however, is not measured by how big is your wallet or the make of car you drive. It can't be given and it can't be taken away. It could only be learned, grasped and grown into.

True wealth is your loved ones, the time you get to spend with family and the breaths you take as you walk through the sand on the beach. It's the memories of your childhood, and of your son or daughter's childhood. It really is bear hugs, kisses, and words like I love you. It's hours in your kitchen baking together with loved ones, accidental spills, and working together to clean it up while having a good laugh. It's the first-time you open your eyes on holiday and understand that you aren't at home. It is a telephone call to someone you care about who lives a long ways away. Wealth can be so many things and so many things aren't true wealth.

It's never too soon to get started on saving in effort to accomplish financial security. Unfortunately, for many individuals the future tends to morph in to the present faster than they ever thought possible. This results in many years of wasted time, leaving people to work well past their retirement age. Don't allow a similar thing to eventually happen to you.

Start paying off debt, saving money, and creating ways to boost your income today. This way you'll be able to build wealth for you and your loved ones.

www.ingramcontent.com/pod-product-compliance
Lightning Source LLC
Chambersburg PA
CBHW081146170526
45158CB00009BA/2728

* 9 781090 841285 *